MEDITATIONS ON CHRIST

MEDITATIONS ON
CHRIST

A 5-Minute Guided Journal
for Christians

Benjamin W. Decker

Illustrations by Gemma Capdevila

ROCKRIDGE
PRESS

To my mother, Karma, and my father, Jeff, for their pure hearts and dedication to our family, to prayer, and to the Holy Spirit. Thank you for raising me in both the spirit and the letter of the law. In so doing, you have given me the world.

For general information on our other products and services or to obtain technical support, please contact our Customer Care Department within the United States at (866) 744-2665, or outside the United States at (510) 253-0500.

Rockridge Press publishes its books in a variety of electronic and print formats. Some content that appears in print may not be available in electronic books, and vice versa.

TRADEMARKS: Rockridge Press and the Rockridge Press logo are trademarks or registered trademarks of Callisto Media Inc. and/or its affiliates, in the United States and other countries, and may not be used without written permission. All other trademarks are the property of their respective owners. Rockridge Press is not associated with any product or vendor mentioned in this book.

Interior and Cover Designer: Jill Lee

Art Producer: Tom Hood

Editor: Andrea Leptinsky

Illustrations ©Gemma Capdevila, 2020; Author photo courtesy of ©Josh Litchman

ISBN: Print 978-1-64611-806-9

R0

"Meditation is the most powerful tool we have for spiritual growth and transformation. Ben Decker's book is a beautiful entrée into the art and ecstasy of practicing the presence of God."

Reverend Michael Bernard Beckwith
Founder & Spiritual Director, Agape International Spiritual Center
Author, *Life Visioning and Spiritual Liberation*

"Ben Decker's teachings are at the forefront of a new age, initiating our generation into a new era of spirituality; where levels of consciousness once attainable only to an elite few are now accessible to everyone within the sound of his voice. His words will change you. Ben is someone I trust completely. I know that God works through him. *Meditations on Christ* is a genuinely prophetic transmission of power and an attunement to a level of Spirit you cannot imagine. Get ready, you're about to shift."

Reverend Donald Guffey
Unifour Christian Fellowship Church

"No one can give us a greater gift than to teach us how to meditate. Many will one day remember Ben Decker [through *Practical Meditation for Beginners*] as having put their feet on a most joyous path."

Marianne Williamson
Author, *A Return to Love* and *Illuminata*

"Sometimes the words we're taught get lost in the redundancy of their repetition. The beauty of Ben Decker's *Meditations on Christ* is its invitation for the reader to take a deeper and more personal look at these commonly known teachings. This book beautifully cultivates a space for insight and introspection. The stillness practices allow these deeper truths to root themselves in the subconscious so that they become not only a practice, but a way of life."

AnnaLynne McCord
Actress, Abolitionist, President of Together 1 Heart

"*Peace I leave with you, my peace I give unto you . . . Let not your heart be troubled, neither let it be afraid.*"

John 14:27
King James Version

This Journal Belongs To:

_____

Contents

Introduction

The goal of *Meditations on Christ* is to deepen our relationship with the Spirit of Jesus Christ and to greater embody His likeness. Meditation is the inner work of self-reflection and self-transformation through mental, physical, and emotional discipline. In Christian meditation, we reflect on Biblical truths and their relevance to our lives. We look to them to help open our hearts and minds so that we may welcome the Spirit's guidance in all of our thoughts, words, and deeds.

Prayer and Meditation

Prayer is the method by which we set the intention in Christian meditation. We give the meditation to the Holy Spirit and welcome the Spirit's presence and guidance. Any time we find that our mind wanders or we go off course in meditation, we come back to that intention as the focal point of the practice.

When we pray, we are often expressing our gratitude, acknowledging our blessings, and praying for support and insight in challenging times. When we meditate, we are listening intentionally to the exchange between the Holy Spirit and ourselves, and we often watch as our thoughts battle with the greater truth of the Spirit. Through disciplined meditation, we begin to tame our lower nature that we might alchemize our darkness and ignorance into light and wisdom.

Meditation is a sacred, ancient practice that people of all world traditions practice in some form or another. Today, modern science has shown meditation to have physiological benefits, such as reduced stress, pain, and inflammation, as well as clearer thinking and a calmer mental attitude. It also has been shown to lead to increased patience, focus, and support for emotional processing, and the list goes on. In addition to these benefits, our meditation practice as Christians is dedicated to three main priorities: welcoming the Holy Spirit, living a more Christlike life, and building His kingdom on Earth as it is in Heaven.

Taking just five minutes to calm the mind, relax the body, observe our thoughts, and listen to the Holy Spirit pierces the veil between the spiritual and physical worlds. The Spirit only needs the smallest amount of openness to enter into our hearts, and five minutes is enough to do just that. If you have more time, I recommend taking as much time in meditation as is comfortable for you. A consistent daily practice of 20 to 40 minutes twice a day is one of the most common recommendations, but don't let that intimidate you. The goal is to simply begin, even if it's just five minutes right now.

> *"Do not despise humble beginnings, for*
> *the LORD rejoices to see the work begin . . . "*
>
> Zechariah 4:10
> *New Living Translation*

In this context, our brief meditation practices constitute our "humble beginnings." It means that the heavens celebrate with you that you are initiating this process, no matter how short or long your practice might be. The depth of your sincerity and openheartedness are the most relevant factors in meditation for spiritual development.

You have been on a journey of learning and growing in the Spirit, and this journal will act as an initiation into the next season of your relationship with the Lord. Open your heart, open your mind, and let the Spirit work with you in quiet moments.

Meditation and prayer work together to facilitate an active two-way relationship between ourselves and God. By adding journaling and reflective writing, we find that the Holy Spirit will use our thoughts and reflections to guide and inspire us, enriching and deepening our understanding of any challenges and difficult circumstances. Allow the Spirit to work through you as you journal.

The Fruit of the Holy Spirit

Throughout our lives, we will often face situations that can be confusing or disturbing. We will also confront tough decisions that can shake our faith. How can we know if our challenges are there to help us grow or if they are signals that we need to make critical changes in our lives? We need the discernment of the Spirit.

Christ is the perfect embodiment of the Spirit of God. He is the Son of God, the miracle worker, the overcomer, the way maker, and our brother. As fellow children of God, our task is to learn more about His character and to become more like Him. *Meditations on Christ* will help us deepen the connection to His qualities and make them our own.

In Matthew 7:20 (King James Version), we are taught a profound secret for discerning of the Spirit: "Where-fore by their fruits ye shall know them." This means that we look to the health of the part (the fruit) to gauge the health of the whole. A healthy tree will bear good fruit; an unhealthy tree will bear low-quality fruit. What does this mean for us?

From Galatians 5:22 (English Standard Version), we know that "the fruit of the Spirit is love, joy, peace, patience, kindness, goodness, faithfulness, gentleness, self-control: against such things there is no law." Through the cultivation of the fruit of the Spirit within our hearts, we begin to experience deeper gifts, including a gift of discernment that provides personal insight and revelation.

Every meditation in *Meditations on Christ* is based on the fruit of the Spirit as found in Galatians. You'll find three meditations for each of these nine qualities as well as a Biblical verse for cross-reference, a unique meditation practice, and journal prompts for self-reflection.

Preparing for Meditation

In today's world, amid the hustle and bustle of everyday pressures and the nonstop digital universe, the idea of a regular meditation practice can seem daunting or even impossible. Let this be easy. Be gentle with yourself.

Set yourself up for success by preparing a sacred space to set the tone for your practice, and it's helpful to establish some level of consistency. For some, that means taking time during their commute to meditate and journal. For others, that means sitting on the back porch early in the morning or meditating for a few minutes on the couch. Still others will have a sacred corner with an altar, including an image of Christ, a few candles, and a place to store your journal. Find a comfortable place, where you have enough privacy to go inward and are unlikely to be interrupted.

The Bible teaches us that prayer is about our own inner relationship with the one true source of all things, our Heavenly Father. This is essentially true about meditation as well. The greatest priority when it comes to prayer and meditation is that we open our hearts as a temple to Christ and welcome the Spirit within. Of course, we often imagine idyllic nature scenes or beautiful sacred buildings and elaborate prayer or meditation closets.

While a dedicated place to hold your practice can be very helpful, it is actually not necessary. As children of God, we are walking portals to the Divine, and the Kingdom of Heaven is within. Through us, the Spirit moves through the Earth, and an important part of the journey of individual spiritual development is learning to create a sacred place with our faith and reverence.

People all over the world choose to meditate in many ways, following a wide variety of recommendations. In Christian meditation, you will rarely find specific prescriptions for posture or what to "do" with your body, as you would in yoga. You may choose to sit cross-legged for your meditation or recline in your favorite chair. In this book, I provide some recommendations for each practice. Some meditations ask you to hold your hands against your heart. Others will suggest holding your hands open in your lap or opening your eyes.

The most important thing is to be comfortable, awake, and relaxed. If that means meditating cross-legged on a cushion with your hands in a yogic mudra, or posture, so be it, but it's not at all necessary. Regardless of your exact posture, the goal is to be focused on the meditation itself, not allowing any discomfort or distractions to pull your mental attention away from your focus on listening to the Holy Spirit's voice.

During his early ministry in Galilee, Christ taught us that we would do greater things than the miracles he performed. As we meditate on God's word and allow ourselves to become more like Him, we will begin to see miracles in our lives, according to our faith. Meditating on these sacred universal principles deepens our faith, and opens our awareness to the important work the Lord is doing in the world through our lives.

Our perspective begins to change when we allow ourselves to be open to seeing the world through the eyes of Christ, rather than through the lens of the material world. Through meditating on Christ and the fruit of the Holy Spirit, we partner with the Great Redeemer and His sacred invocation in the Garden of Gethsemane. As our minds turn to thoughts of Heaven, we open ourselves to God and cocreating His kingdom on Earth. We look at our spiritual principles as an invisible, metaphysical blueprint for the inner foundation that allows us to build a sacred outer world.

The brief time for your practice should be dedicated solely to your meditation. It is not the time to solve all of your problems. **The miracle of the meditation often happens afterward, out in the world, while living our lives.** If unpleasant feelings, memories, or experiences arise in your heart or mind during meditation, always remember that in the presence of the Holy Spirit, nothing is insurmountable and nothing is impossible. We dedicate our hearts as sacred temples to the Holy Spirit and invite the infinite power of God to grant us with the peace that surpasses understanding. When challenging thoughts arise in meditation, breathe through them in the faith that all things can and will be transformed for good.

How to Use This Journal

Look at this journal as a tool to help you as you embody Christlike characteristics in your life. Each meditation is based on a Bible verse to help you set a prayerful intention for the practice, followed by a meditation exercise and journal writing prompts. In Mark 2:27 (New International Version), Christ says, "The Sabbath was made for man, not man for the Sabbath," and the same is true for this journal. The journal was made for you, not you for the journal, which means that you are invited to let your own intuition guide you in exactly how to work with these prompts. As you write, try to focus your attention on the subject at hand. This helps cultivate and sustain the meditation benefits of clearer thinking and increased focus.

Bible Translations

There are many different English translations of the Holy Bible, and communities find themselves gravitating toward a particular one. For our purposes, each passage has been prayerfully curated from a number of translations, including the King James Version, the Revised Standard Version, the New International Version, and a number of others.

LOVE

If there is one concept that Jesus Christ embodied and taught above all others, it is love. This section will include prompts and practices that tune our hearts to the Divine Love of the Lord. We can emanate the Lord's love of all by welcoming Him into our hearts and allowing His ways to become our own.

Love: The Greatest Commandment

"'Love the LORD your God with all your heart and with all your soul and with all your mind.' This is the first and greatest commandment. And the second is like it: 'Love your neighbor as yourself.' All the Law and the Prophets hang on these two commandments."

Matthew 22:37–40
New International Version

Prayer and Meditation

Say a brief prayer to set the intention for your meditation:

"Dear God, thank You for this day and for all of the blessings I enjoy. Please fill me with Your Holy Spirit now as I meditate to cultivate love for You and all of Your children with all of my heart, soul, and mind. I ask this in the name of Jesus Christ. Amen."

Sit quietly and allow your body to rest in relaxed stillness.

Place both hands over your heart and breathe, feeling God's love flow in and out of your heart with every beat and with every breath.

Open your thoughts and feelings and allow God's voice to enter your being.

With every inhale, silently repeat, "Love for God. My neighbor. Myself."

With every exhale, silently repeat, "Heart. Soul. Mind."

Often when we begin the process of cultivating Divine Love in our hearts, we are quickly reminded of something or someone considered unlovable by ordinary human standards. To love someone (or to receive Christ's love for ourselves) is not the same as condoning dysfunctional behavior. To love someone is to see beyond behavior to the purity of the soul within.

What are some ways you can allow yourself to experience the love of Christ today? In what ways, if any, have you been withholding yourself from the experience of God's love? Be sure to write from a place of faith, knowing that you are deeply loved by your Heavenly Family.

What are some ways you can begin to express the love of Christ to your neighbor (friend, coworker, family member, etc.) today? In what ways, if any, have you been withholding love from others? Write from a perspective of compassion and mercy, remembering Christ's infinite mercy and love.

The Qualities of Love

*"Love is patient and kind; love is not
jealous or boastful; it is not arrogant or rude.
Love does not insist on its own way; it is not
irritable or resentful; it does not rejoice at wrong,
but rejoices in the right. Love bears all things,
believes all things, hopes all things, endures all
things."*

1 Corinthians 13:4–7
Revised Standard Version

Prayer and Meditation

Say a brief prayer to set the intention for your meditation:

"Dear God, thank You for this day and the blessings that surround me. Your presence is welcome here now as I meditate on the qualities of true love found in Corinthians. Please guide my practice. I ask this in the name of Jesus Christ. Amen."

Sit quietly and allow your body to rest in relaxed stillness.

Place both hands open in your lap, as if you are receiving a gift.

Breathe naturally, allowing your body to relax.

Allow your thoughts and feelings to let God's voice enter your being.

Visualize Christ Jesus inside every part of your body, every part of your soul, and every part of your mind. Allow His presence within you to attune your qualities to His.

To accept Christ Jesus into our hearts is to accept His heart as our own. These powerful verses in Corinthians lead us to the secrets and qualities of Christ's heart. By allowing Him to be fully present within us, overshadowing our own characteristics and qualities, we create space for His love to move through us, healing and transforming us at our very core.

Affirmations are positive statements of truth, such as "I am
_____, even in_____ ." This trains the mind and the heart to
take on these qualities and directs our thoughts and imagina-
tions to support them. Take this moment to write affirmations in
present tense about yourself to cultivate love. Feel free to use
real-life examples, letting the Spirit guide you.

Examples: *I am loving, even in the midst of frustrating
conversations with coworkers. I am loving, even in the midst
of stressful conditions in high-pressure circumstances.*

The material world is the exact opposite of God's kingdom. We see symbols of wealth lauded here as keys to happiness and success, but those who know the Spirit know the truth: Nothing in the material world can truly satisfy. This is why it's so important to reflect on the ways we are jealous, boastful, irritable, or resentful, clearing them from our hearts and minds with the help of the Holy Spirit.

Using your journal space, reflect on how you have acted in these ways. Forgive yourself and others in the process. Be as specific as you like, but remember to let the Spirit lead, always writing from a Christlike perspective and being very gentle with your shortcomings and those of others.

The Power of Love

"There is no fear in love. But perfect love drives out fear, because fear has to do with punishment. The one who fears is not made perfect in love."

1 John 4:18
New International Version

Prayer and Meditation

Say a brief prayer to set the intention for your meditation:

"Dear God, thank You for this day and all that You have given me. I ask for the Holy Spirit to be present with me now as I meditate on the perfect love that casts out all fear. Please lead me, guide me, and show me the way. I ask this in the name of Jesus Christ. Amen."

Sit quietly and allow your body to rest in relaxed stillness.

Place both hands open in your lap, as if you are receiving a gift.

Breathe naturally, allowing your body to relax.

Allow yourself to open, letting God's voice enter your mind and heart.

Visualize yourself glowing in a white light that symbolizes perfect love.

Visualize any fears or uncertainties as shadows, cast out of your heart, mind, and soul by the light of perfect love.

Allowing ourselves to radiate with perfect light guides us toward perfect love. Where there is light, there is no longer darkness. Where there is perfect love, fear no longer exists.

Where in your life do you see shadows of fear? Write about them faithfully, knowing that the perfect love of Christ shining from within you casts out all fears. Do you see any fearful circumstances differently as a result of opening yourself to greater love?

Opening our hearts and minds to different ways of seeing and feeling is crucial for allowing the Holy Spirit to give us the miracle we need. This also means that we must fully accept Christ's atonement and become one with Him, allowing ourselves to fully receive His eternal forgiveness and mercy. Without the full acceptance of that forgiveness and mercy, we will be left with fear, which belongs to the enemy.

Do you fear punishment in any areas of your life? Do you feel you have yet to be cleansed of anything and forgiven? Take this moment now to accept the forgiveness Christ offers you. Journal about the changes and healing that have taken place (or that you hope to take place) as a result of being made perfect in love.

JOY

God's will is for us to have total fulfillment and joy, and this comes from a supernatural understanding and transcendental faith. This section will help us cultivate that faith, creating the possibility for spiritual encounters with God and feelings of inexpressible and glorious joy.

Face to Face with God

"I have much to write to you, but I do not want to use paper and ink. Instead, I hope to visit you and talk with you face to face, so that our joy may be complete."

2 John 1:12
New International Version

Prayer and Meditation

Say a brief prayer to set the intention for your meditation:

"Dear God, thank You for this day and this sacred journey of learning. Please help me feel the presence of the Holy Spirit now as I meditate on You and Your word "that our joy may be complete." I ask for a glimpse of personal face-to-face experience with You now. Please guide my practice. I ask and pray for these things in the name of Jesus Christ. Amen."

Sit quietly and allow your body to rest in relaxed stillness.

Place both hands open in your lap, as if you are receiving a gift.

Breathe naturally, allowing your body to relax and bringing awareness back to your breath if your mind begins to wander.

Visualize Christ Jesus sitting directly across from you, looking at you with great love, great happiness, and perfect tenderness.

Receive the gift of His presence as if He really did miraculously appear in front of you to silently show you His love.

One of our greatest practices is that of increasing our awareness of God's presence. When we are swept up in the drama of normal life, forgetting God's presence, we often fall out of the joy of living. He is always here, and it is up to us to become aware of His presence, which brings joy to even the simplest moments.

What came to mind as you meditated? Were you able to maintain your focus on your breath and the encounter, or did you find it challenging? How did the presence of the Spirit feel? Write here about the experience and any particular insights you gleaned from your visualization.

Reflect on your day-to-day life. What kinds of things prevent you from being aware of God's presence? What are some ways you can invite the Spirit into your life?

Transcendental Faith

"Consider it pure joy, my brothers and sisters, whenever you face trials of many kinds, because you know that the testing of your faith produces perseverance."

James 1:2–3
New International Version

Prayer and Meditation

Say a brief prayer to set the intention for your meditation:

"Dear God, thank You for this day and the opportunity to increase my faith. Give me strength in the face of my trials, for I know that You are always with me. Your presence is welcome here now as I meditate on the pure joy of knowing that my faith in You and in truth increases as I overcome my challenges. Please guide my practice. I ask this in the name of my brother, Jesus Christ. Amen."

Sit quietly and allow your body to rest in relaxed stillness.

Rest your hands face down on your thighs.

Take a few deep breaths, then breathe naturally, allowing your body to rest.

Allow your thoughts and feelings to invite the Spirit into your being, while maintaining your stillness.

Visualize Christ Jesus inside your heart, mind, soul, and body, and contemplate your most immediate challenges.

Breathe deeply as you visualize yourself surrendering to Christ within, allowing Him to navigate these challenges on your behalf.

The foundational principle here is that God is not only with us at all times, but also that He is all-powerful, all-loving, all-intelligent, and totally faithful to us and our needs. If something in our lives is important to us, it's important to Him. If something causes us concern or worry, we must always remember that He is there for us. We can give Him the worries of our hearts, freeing us to feel joy.

When has your faith been tested? What were the circumstances, and did some challenges seem insurmountable? As you recall these situations, write about what happened. Focus on the outcome found in the present moment, interpreting it as positively as possible.

Now, write about your current challenges. As you write, choose your words thoughtfully. Are they positive and hopeful, or are they heavy or negative? Try to adjust your attitude to an empowered, faithful, positive one. Be as faithful as possible as you write, knowing that our faith gives us hope our challenges will be overcome.

Inexpressible and Glorious Joy

"Though you have not seen him, you love him;
and even though you do not see him now, you
believe in him and are filled with an inexpressible
and glorious joy, for you are receiving the end
result of your faith, the salvation of your souls."

1 Peter 1:8–9
New International Version

Prayer and Meditation

Say a brief prayer to set the intention for your meditation:

"Dear God, thank You for this day and the blessings that surround me. Please fill my heart and mind with Your Holy Spirit as I meditate on the inexpressible and glorious joy Peter speaks of. Please show me what salvation really means. Speak to me as I meditate. I ask this in the name of Jesus Christ. Amen."

Sit quietly and allow your body to rest in relaxed stillness.

Place both hands open in your lap, as if you are receiving a gift.

Breathe naturally, allowing your body to relax.

Smile, and open your mind and heart to joy and the blessings of God.

Recall some of your deepest, happiest experiences, expanding those memories to imagine a joy beyond description.

Breathe joy into every cell of your body, maintaining a smile for the duration of the meditation.

Sometimes we can find it hard to smile when we aren't immediately aware of "something to smile about." We must train ourselves to remember that the blessings of God surround us at all times, even when we can't see them. The cultivation of joy is not just for its own sake. Remember, this is the fruit of the Spirit, which means that we are cultivating something deeper—a relationship with the Spirit, and joy is one of the indications of actual contact with the Spirit.

Joy and fun are very different qualities. It doesn't mean that they can't exist together; actually, they often do. Fun exists on a more material, physical level. Joy manifests as a higher, spiritual quality, beyond physical circumstances.

There is great joy in some of the simplest experiences. What brings you joy? Write down as many things as you can.

The joy described by Peter is "inexpressible and glorious," suggesting that it is beyond human description. Prophets have used metaphors and symbols to describe the bliss of a Holy Encounter and the liberation and salvation of the personal soul. Take some time now to describe what the experience of salvation means for you. Open your heart and mind, remembering that although we may try to describe such a profound ecstatic experience, words will never be enough.

PEACE

The peace brought by the Holy Spirit is far beyond anything the world could ever provide. In this section, we will affirm sacred truths, remind ourselves of the great blessings we have, and strengthen our courage in the face of uncertainty that we might experience the presence of the Spirit directly. Order is brought into even the most extraordinary chaos, through the peace of God.

Let Not Your Heart Be Troubled

"Peace I leave with you; My peace I give unto you; not as the world gives do I give to you. Let not your heart be troubled, neither let it be afraid."

John 14:27
New King James Version

Prayer and Meditation

Say a brief prayer to set the intention for your meditation:

"Dear God, thank You for this day and the peace that You have brought to this world. Please help me become more and more aware of Your presence now and always. I place my fears in Your hands and know that You will turn them to faith and love. I hand You the troubles of my heart, for I know that You are all-powerful and unstoppable. Please guide my practice. I ask this in the name of Jesus Christ. Amen."

Sit quietly and allow your body to rest in relaxed stillness.

Place both hands over your heart and breathe, feeling God's peace flow in and out with every beat and with every breath.

Breathe naturally, allowing your body to relax.

Allow yourself to open, silently repeating the phrase "God's peace is here now."

Repeat the phrase, as needed, when your mind wanders and you need to refocus.

Our world has a collective understanding of peace, which relies on calm or easy circumstances, but God is not from this world. He created it. His extraordinary peace is far beyond anything that comes from peace here, which is based on ever-changing external circumstances. The peace of God, however, is constant and never-ending and comes from an internal awareness of God's eternal presence.

Reflect on the troubles of your heart. Write them down, adding the phrase, "God has given me His peace, even in _____."

Examples:
God has given me His peace, even in my uncertainty about my job.
God has given me His peace, even in the challenges of my relationship.
God has given me His peace, even in my financial concerns.

Now, reflect on the troubles of your heart and write them down, adding the phrase, "My heart is not troubled, nor is it afraid in the _____."

Examples:
My heart is not troubled, nor is it afraid in the uncertainty about my job.
My heart is not troubled, nor is it afraid in the challenges of my relationship.
My heart is not troubled, nor is it afraid in my financial concerns.

The Peace Which Surpasses All Understanding

> *"And the peace of God, which surpasses all understanding, will guard your hearts and minds in Christ Jesus."*

Philippians 4:7
Christian Standard Bible

Prayer and Meditation

Say a brief prayer to set the intention for your meditation:

"Dear God, thank You for this day and the blessings that surround me. Guard my heart with Your peace. Guard my mind with Your peace. I invite the Holy Spirit into the darkest places within me, that they may be made light. Please be with me now and guide my practice. I ask this in the name of Jesus Christ. Amen."

Sit quietly and allow your body to rest in relaxed stillness.

Place both hands open in your lap, as if you are receiving a gift.

Breathe naturally, allowing your body to relax.

Visualize yourself in an invisible force field of angelic protection.

Open yourself to the sounds and movements you hear in all directions around you, without reacting.

After the meditation, take that invisible force field of angelic protection with you wherever you go.

We are liberated when we open our hearts and minds, actively inviting the Spirit to be with us and surrendering our personal ambitions to His guidance. The peace that "surpasses understanding" is a peace that others around us may not even understand. Remember that field of protection. Inside that field lives the Holy Spirit.

Remember a time when you felt peace. Write a letter of gratitude to God about the ways that you've experienced His peace and how it felt.

Write a letter to yourself to refer to in a moment of crisis. Remind your future self that the Holy Spirit is there to lead, guide, and protect you, even in the face of great uncertainty and concern.

Peace and Order

"For God is not a God of disorder but of peace—
as in all the congregations of the LORD's people."

1 Corinthians 14:33
New International Version

Prayer and Meditation

Say a brief prayer to set the intention for your meditation:

"Dear God, thank You for this day and the blessings that surround me. Your presence is welcome here now as I meditate on order. Let there be order and clarity in my mind. Let there be order and health in my body. Let there be order and love in my relationships. Please guide my practice. Grant me with Your wisdom and insight. I ask this in the name of Jesus Christ. Amen."

Sit quietly and allow your body to rest in relaxed stillness.

Take a few deep breaths, then breathe naturally.

In your mind's eye, visualize a spark of golden light, symbolizing your spirit—the deepest part of you that is divine, that has never left God.

Visualize the light shining from the core of your being, guided by the Holy Spirit. Begin to see that light rearrange your thoughts, changing your mental habits and behaviors and calling them into perfect, divine order.

See the light shining through your body, calling every cell and organ into perfect health.

Finally, see the endless light shine in all directions around you as you visualize order in your home, your city, your nation, and all over the world.

It is said that "cleanliness is next to Godliness, but order is divine." When we "clean house" spiritually, we begin to find that a kind of "reset" begins to occur. We may choose to fast, change our diets, clean our homes, organize our closets, and clear the air in our relationships. These are outer expressions that can come from various inner impulses, but when they are prompted by the Holy Spirit, they bring sacredness to the world around us.

How can you bring order to your inner world? How can you be more consistent with your prayer and meditation practice, infusing every moment of the day with prayer? What does that look like for you?

How can you bring increased order into your external world? Are there relationships that need to be recalibrated? Are there areas of clutter in your home or workspace that you can sort and organize? Describe what it looks like for you to bring order into the world around you.

PATIENCE

Navigating the rough seas of life can be impossible without the patience brought on by the Spirit. Patience is an example of spiritual maturity, and we develop that maturity only through experience. In this section, we will slow down, let the Spirit lead, and accept things as they are, releasing our anxiety to God.

Do Not Be Provoked

"Do not let yourself be quickly provoked, for anger resides in the lap of fools."

Ecclesiastes 7:9
New English Translation

Prayer and Meditation

Say a brief prayer to set the intention for your meditation:

"Dear God, thank You for this day and the great peace that Your Holy Spirit gives never-endingly. Let me always remember Your presence, for You are eternally present with me in every moment. I give this meditation to You. Please plant Your patience both in my heart and as a shield around me, that I may not be provoked to anger. I desire only to be wise and never foolish. Be with me now as I meditate. I ask this in the name of Jesus Christ. Amen."

Sit quietly and allow your body to rest in relaxed stillness.

Place both hands open in your lap, as if you are receiving a gift.

Breathe naturally, allowing your body to relax.

Allow your thoughts and feelings to open to the Spirit and relax.

Visualize Christ Jesus inside every part of your body, soul, and mind, and allow His presence within you to attune your qualities to His.

Take a moment to reflect on your relationship to anger. Describe a moment when you became angry. How did it feel? What would you do differently?

Write down a prayer of your own, perhaps inspired by the prayers in this book, asking God to be as present as possible with you in challenging times. Be as specific as possible with your request.

Bountiful Harvest

"Let us not become weary in doing good, for at the proper time we will reap a harvest if we do not give up."

Galatians 6:9
New International Version

Prayer and Meditation

Say a brief prayer to set the intention for your meditation:

"Dear God, thank You for this day. Lord, You are ruler of all things on Earth and Heaven. May I always remember this deep truth. May I be diligent, consistent, and patient in Your work as I await Your bountiful harvest. Please speak to me as I meditate to deeply establish a sense of sacred patience in my heart, mind, and soul. I ask this in the name of Jesus Christ. Amen."

Sit quietly and allow your body to rest in relaxed stillness.

Place both hands open in your lap, as if you are receiving a gift.

Breathe naturally, allowing your body to relax and your thoughts and feelings to flow freely.

Visualize yourself as loving and generous.

Think specifically about the people in your life, and your acting perfectly loving and generous toward them.

Can you think of individuals who are good examples of generosity? In what ways are they generous? Be detailed as you write this down.

In what areas of your life do you feel you could be more patient? Write down specific circumstances when you will choose to be more patient.

_____

_____

_____

_____

_____

_____

_____

_____

_____

_____

_____

_____

_____

_____

_____

_____

_____

_____

Releasing Anxiety

"Be anxious for nothing, but in everything by prayer and supplication, with thanksgiving, let your requests be made known to God."

Philippians 4:6
New King James Version

Prayer and Meditation

Say a brief prayer to set the intention for your meditation:

"Dear God, thank You for this day and the blessings that fill my life and the lives of those I love. Be with me in this meditation now, as I open my heart and mind to remembering that I am Your child, whom You love forever and always. Let me remember Your generosity with gratitude and thanksgiving. Bless me now in all of the ways You know I need most. I ask this in the name of Jesus Christ. Amen."

Sit quietly and allow your body to rest in relaxed stillness.

Place both hands open in your lap, as if you are receiving a gift.

Breathe naturally, allowing your body to rest.

Let God's voice fully enter your heart and mind.

With every exhale, allow every muscle of your body to more deeply relax as you silently repeat the phrase "Ah, thank you. Yes."

Cultivate a sense of gratitude as you continue to silently repeat the phrase "Ah, thank you. Yes."

Write down your blessings, beginning with the phrase, "I am so happy and grateful for _____."

Examples:
I am so happy and grateful for the safety I am experiencing in the present moment.
I am so happy and grateful for the overall health and strength of my body.
I am so happy and grateful for the fact that I have overcome so many challenges.

Now, write down some of the blessings you gratefully anticipate, using the previous phrase and ending it with "_____ coming to me now." Avoid anything materialistic, unless it is absolutely necessary for your well-being.

Examples:
I am so happy and grateful for the financial breakthrough coming to me now.
I am so happy and grateful for the spiritual insight and wisdom coming to me now.
I am so happy and grateful for the greater health and fitness coming to me now.

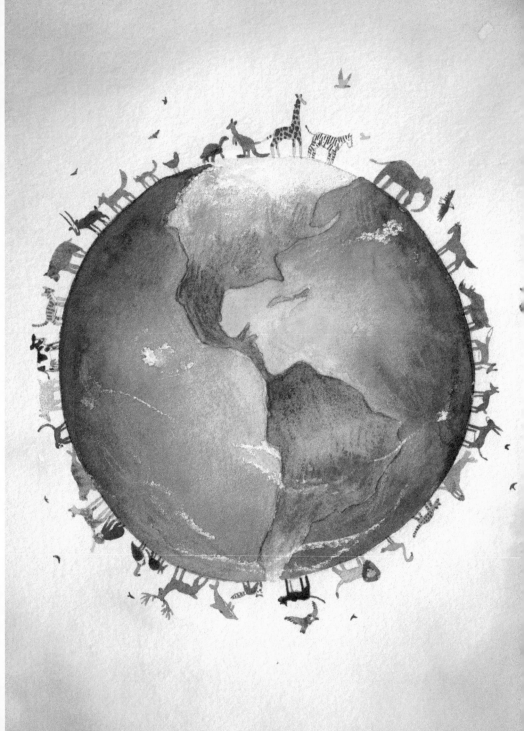

KINDNESS

Often, it is believed that kindness is about the effect we have on others, but the Spirit teaches us that being kind benefits our own hearts as well. In the spiritual world, that which we give, we also receive. In this section, we will remind ourselves that we are all family in the Kingdom of God, and that every last one of us deserves the lovingkindness of mercy and compassion.

Benefits of Kindness

"A kind man benefits himself, but a cruel person brings ruin on himself."

Proverbs 11:17
Christian Standard Bible

Prayer and Meditation

Say a brief prayer to set the intention for your meditation:

"Dear God, thank You for this day and the beautiful world You have created for my benefit and learning. Protect me from cruelty and bless me with the spiritual gift of kindness. May I be more like Your son, my brother, the Christ. Reveal to me in this meditation my unity with all of Your children, so that Your kindness may flow from me to them naturally and effortlessly. I ask this in the name of Jesus Christ. Amen."

Sit quietly and allow your body to rest in relaxed stillness.

Place both hands over your heart.

Allow your heart and mind to open as thoughts and feelings arise, breathing through them.

Cultivate a sense of lovingkindness in your heart.

Silently repeat the phrase "God's kindness passes through me to those around me."

Call to mind the people in your life, and those with whom you have difficulty, as you continue to repeat the phrase "God's kindness passes through me to those around me."

In God's kingdom, all people are members of His royal family, and our work is to build His kingdom on Earth, as it is in Heaven. Kindness is one of the most meaningful and powerful gifts we can give one another along the way.

In God's kingdom, we are all brothers and sisters. To love someone and to be kind to them does not mean condoning any harmful or abusive behavior. On the contrary, we condemn negative behavior while maintaining our commitment to love and kindness. If Christ were to return, with His infinite love and mercy, what kinds of changes might we see in the world today?

What does "heavenly" mean to you? In what ways could you help make the world a more heavenly place?

_____

_____

_____

_____

_____

_____

_____

_____

_____

_____

_____

_____

_____

_____

_____

_____

_____

_____

Love in Deed and in Truth

*"My little children, let us not love in word,
neither in tongue; but in deed and in truth."*

1 John 3:18
King James Version

Prayer and Meditation

Say a brief prayer to set the intention for your meditation:

"Dear God, thank You for this day and the sacred miracle of life. Every day is a blessing, and I know You are helping me understand that. I invite the Holy Spirit to be more present than ever with me now, so that I may gain insight and wisdom. Let Your love be made manifest not only through my words, but also through my deeds. I ask this in the name of Jesus Christ. Amen."

Sit quietly and allow your body to rest in stillness.

Place both hands over your heart and breathe, feeling God's love flow in and out of your heart with every beat and with every breath.

Try to open your thoughts and feelings to accept the Spirit with your whole being.

Visualize Christ Jesus inside your body, soul, and mind.

See yourself going through the day, allowing Christ within to anoint your actions with love.

What day-to-day activities came to mind during your meditation? Did Christ's love change any of the ways you went about your day? How?

_____

_____

_____

_____

_____

_____

_____

_____

_____

_____

_____

_____

_____

_____

_____

As you visualize Christ inside every part of you, what are some of the thoughts that come to mind? What kinds of changes might He make to your inner world if you gave Him the opportunity?

Show Mercy and Compassion

"Thus says the LORD of hosts, Render true judgments, show kindness and mercy to one another, do not oppress the widow, the fatherless, the sojourner, or the poor, and let none of you devise evil against another in your heart."

Zechariah 7:9-10
English Standard Version

Prayer and Meditation

Say a brief prayer to set the intention for your meditation:

"Dear God, thank You for this day. Thank You for the mercy and grace that You have shown me. Let my heart be softened that I might learn the nature of Your compassion, that I may become more and more like You with every breath I take and with each day that I live. I ask this in the name of Jesus Christ. Amen."

Sit quietly and allow your body to rest in relaxed stillness.

Place both hands open in your lap, as if you are receiving a gift.

Breathe naturally, allowing your body to relax.

Call to mind any times when you have been unkind or unloving, and visualize yourself giving these situations to Jesus Christ.

Breathe through any uncomfortable feelings, knowing that Jesus is infinitely merciful, forgiving, and loving.

Christ has said that He will return to Earth, and we are asked to prepare the way by preparing ourselves. To ready ourselves and the world for His triumphant reign and an era of peace, we are asked to change our minds, our hearts, and our behavior.

What are some ways that you can show mercy, compassion, and kindness in your personal life? Write down things that you already do, but also write down what you can begin to practice now.

How can society as a whole begin to show greater mercy, compassion, and kindness?

_____

_____

_____

_____

_____

_____

_____

_____

_____

_____

_____

_____

_____

_____

_____

GOODNESS

In a world that so often shows us chaos and drama, it is only those who live in the Spirit who can discern the goodness that truly does surround us. In this section, we will practice seeing the goodness of God, speaking of the goodness of God, and living in a state of gratitude. We will deepen our testimony that God has a Great Plan, and that we have the power to walk with Him in it.

The Goodness of God

> *"Oh, that men would give thanks to*
> *the LORD for His goodness, And for His wonderful*
> *works to the children of men!"*

> Psalm 107:8
> *New King James Version*

Prayer and Meditation

Say a brief prayer to set the intention for your meditation:

"Dear God, thank You for this day. I invite Your spirit to be with me as I meditate on Your goodness. I ask that You show me Your goodness in this meditation today and throughout my life that I may praise You for it. I ask and pray this in the name of Jesus Christ. Amen."

Sit comfortably.

Stretch your body and take a few deep breaths to help you settle in.

With every exhale, silently repeat the sentence "God, show me Your goodness in my life."

Open yourself to the thoughts and images that the Spirit places in your mind, and remain still for the duration of your meditation.

Always redirect your attention back to the breath, and to the focus statement "God, show me Your goodness in my life."

To "give thanks to the Lord for His goodness . . . to the children of men" means to think and speak positively about the inherent goodness of the universe, especially in our interactions with others. God is good all the time. The following journal prompts are intended to support us as we reflect on what that means.

One of the most powerful ways we can praise God's goodness is through gratitude. Write down things for which you are grateful using the following format: I see the goodness of God in

_____.

Examples:
I see the goodness of God in the beautiful flowers growing in the park near my home.
I see the goodness of God in the love I have for my friends and family.
I see the goodness of God in new innovations that are making the world a better place.

Take a moment to freewrite a letter of gratitude, praising God's goodness. How does His goodness make you feel? How do you feel blessed by it? Be as detailed as possible.

God's Plan

"So we are convinced that every detail of our lives is continually woven together to fit into God's perfect plan of bringing good into our lives, for we are his lovers who have been called to fulfill his designed purpose."

Romans 8:28
The Passion Translation

Prayer and Meditation

Say a brief prayer to set the intention for your meditation:

"Dear God, thank You for this day. Thank You for calling me to Your great purpose. Please be with me as I meditate today. Deepen my love for You, deepen my awareness of Your purpose, that we may work together for Your good. I ask and pray this in the name of Your son, Jesus Christ. Amen."

Sit comfortably and let yourself relax.

Take a few deep breaths. Let your inhales be full and complete, as well as your exhales; allow your breath to move continuously in and out.

Rest your hands flat in your lap.

Visualize Jesus standing behind you with both of His hands resting gently on your head as He blesses you with insight on God's purpose and plan for His children.

Open your heart and mind as you listen to His words.

We are blessed with free will and the power to creatively express our uniqueness. In what ways do you express your creativity? In what ways can your creative expressions glorify God and bless His children, your brothers and sisters?

The Lord has a Great Plan, and that plan is for the learning, healing, growing, and happiness of all of His children. Can you think of ways to partner with Him toward that end? What might your role look like?

Prayer Walk

> *"Surely goodness and mercy shall follow me all the days of my life: and I shall dwell in the house of the LORD forever."*

Psalm 23:6
Berean Study Bible

Prayer and Meditation

Say a brief prayer to set the intention for your meditation:

"Dear God, thank You for this day. Thank You for Your goodness and Your mercy. Bless me as I meditate today that my mind may be transformed into Your house. Show me evidence and signs of Your goodness and mercy. Fill me with Your spirit as I meditate now. I ask and pray in the name of Jesus Christ. Amen."

Perform this meditation on a casual stroll outdoors, if possible.

As you walk, breathe deeply and open yourself to your surroundings and allow your mind and heart to accept God's voice.

Silently repeat the sentence "Goodness and mercy follow me everywhere I go."

Allow space in your mind for His words to enter.

Envision everyone and everything you pass being blessed by goodness and mercy.

When you finish your walk, have a seat to complete the following journal prompts.

How did your vision of goodness and mercy change the world around you? What do you think those changes symbolize?

_____

_____

_____

_____

_____

_____

_____

_____

_____

_____

_____

_____

_____

_____

_____

_____

_____

_____

How can you share God's goodness and mercy with others? Can you apply these ideas to real-life situations, with specific examples?

_____

_____

_____

_____

_____

_____

_____

_____

_____

_____

_____

_____

_____

_____

_____

_____

_____

FAITHFULNESS

Looking to our brother, Jesus, we find the perfected example of true faithfulness. He is the greatest miracle worker of all time, the God of Love, and the way-shower. In this section, we will be attuned to the frequency of his extraordinary faith, allowing it to become our own, stepping into a New Day.

Spiritual Awakening

"Jesus said this and then added, 'Our friend Lazarus has fallen asleep, but I will go and wake him up.'"

John 11:11
Good News Translation

Prayer and Meditation

Say a brief prayer to set the intention for your meditation:

"Dear God, thank You for this day. Thank You for Your son Jesus Christ and the extraordinary love and faithfulness He showed us in His ministry on Earth. Thank You for His authority over disease, sickness, and death, as shown in the miracle of raising Lazarus from the dead. May I be blessed with faith and awakening as I meditate now. I ask this in the name of Jesus Christ. Amen."

Sit down and take a few deep breaths.

Let your body become still.

Rest your hands open in your lap to receive.

Silently repeat the sentence "Holy Spirit, I am open to seeing things differently."

Watch your thoughts closely as they pass through your mind. Do not dwell on any particular thoughts, always returning to the sentence "Holy Spirit, I am open to seeing things differently."

Christ's love for Lazarus moved Him to perform the miracle of raising him from the dead. He knew Lazarus was dead, but instead referred to it as "sleep." His faith that this was possible is shown in the subtle confidence of this scripture.

How can your faith spark miraculous experiences, either in your life or those of your loved ones?

_____

_____

_____

_____

_____

_____

_____

_____

_____

_____

_____

_____

_____

_____

_____

_____

_____

We are often not called to perform miracles like raising the dead, but we are called to overcome the challenges in our lives. Choose one of your greatest challenges. Write about it now, but with the same attitude of great faith that Jesus had in John 11:11.

Strengthening Your Testimony

"All the paths of the LORD are steadfast love and faithfulness, for those who keep his covenant and his testimonies."

Psalm 25:10
English Standard Version

Prayer and Meditation

Say a brief prayer to set the intention for your meditation:

"Dear God, thank You for this day. It is my intention to honor my covenant with You that my testimony of Your faithfulness may be strengthened. Fill my heart and mind with Your Holy Spirit in this meditation now. Show me Your presence. Allow me to feel Your presence. Influence my thoughts that I may think the thoughts of Heaven. I ask this in the name of Jesus Christ. Amen."

Get into a comfortable seated position and hold your hands over your heart.

Take a few deep breaths and notice the thoughts arising in your mind.

Silently repeat the sentence "Holy Spirit, I am listening only to You."

A covenant is a promise we make with God and with others in the community of faith. What covenant can you enter into with God that will grow your faith in His love and abundance?

Write your testimony of the faithfulness of God. Use a personal example of how He has fulfilled His promises in your life.

Every Day Is a New Day

"You intended to harm me, but God intended it all for good. He brought me to this position so I could save the lives of many people."

Genesis 50:20
New Living Translation

Prayer and Meditation

Say a brief prayer to set the intention for your meditation:

"Dear God, thank You for this day. Thank You that You take what the enemy meant for evil and turn it for good. Please have Your spirit with me as I meditate today. Show me the areas in my life that the enemy meant for evil, and how You will turn it for good. I ask this in the name of Jesus Christ. Amen."

Sit comfortably and contemplate the words of the prayer.

Breathe naturally.

Rest your hands either facing down or facing up in your lap.

Silently repeat this sentence to yourself "What the enemy meant for evil, God will turn for good."

As you meditate, you may be impressed with different thoughts coming to your mind. Sometimes you will see immediate responses from the Holy Spirit, and sometimes you won't. Be patient with yourself and your relationship with the Spirit. Be faithful and willing to hear.

What life challenges came to mind that the Spirit inspired you to turn into good?

_____

_____

_____

_____

_____

_____

_____

_____

_____

_____

_____

_____

_____

_____

_____

_____

_____

_____

Freewrite for a few minutes about the different challenges you face. When you are finished, write the sentence "God, I surrender these challenges to You. I know that You will turn them all for good. Thank You very much."

GENTLENESS

The Spirit will lead our words and actions, gently purifying any harshness from our personalities—if we allow it. Remembering our own imperfections, and the great infinite generosity of compassion God has for us, we will practice being more like Him, extending the same to our sisters and brothers around us. In this section, we will also activate the great power of encouragement, self-initiating into the path of the miracle worker.

Look to Yourself

"Brethren, if a man is overtaken in any trespass, you who are spiritual restore such a one in a spirit of gentleness, considering yourself lest you also be tempted."

Galatians 6:1
New King James Version

Prayer and Meditation

Say a brief prayer to set the intention for your meditation:

"Dear God, thank You for this day. Thank You for Your grace. Thank You for Your infinite and eternal love. Thank You that Your love makes all things new. Bless me that I may learn by the example of Your son Jesus Christ, that I may be loving and gentle, as He is. Reveal to me Your spiritual gifts that I may forgive others their trespasses as You forgive me of mine. Thank You very much. I ask this in the name of Jesus Christ. Amen."

Sit comfortably and begin meditating.

Envision Jesus Christ in your heart, in your mind, and in every part of your body, as if He is attuning the atomic structure of your being to become identical to His.

Bring to mind those individuals with whom you have difficulty in life. You may choose to bring to mind someone who you are frustrated with, someone who has offended you, or even public figures you don't like.

Begin to see them through the loving eyes of Christ.

Notice in the verse that it says, if someone is "overtaken in any trespass." This is forgiving, because it assumes the innocence of the soul underneath the mistaken behavior.

Who came to mind during the meditation? Describe how your thoughts and feelings about them may have become more Christlike as a result of the meditation.

List out anyone who you are worried about, who you care for and love, who has offended you, and who you would like to experience amends with. Write anyone who comes to mind. There is no need to indicate what your feelings are about them, just write out their names, filling up the space provided.

Rejoice

"Rejoice in the LORD always. I will say it again: Rejoice! Let your gentleness be apparent to all. The LORD is near."

Philippians 4:4–5
Berean Study Bible

Prayer and Meditation

Say a brief prayer to set the intention for your meditation:

"Dear God, thank You for this day. May I be blessed with the dignity, gentleness, and moderation of Your ways. May my feet be guided on Your path, and may I be granted insight as I reflect on Your words. May all of my relationships be illuminated with Your truth. May my attitude be one of joy, that I may be a positive influence on all those with whom I interact. Bless me that I may know how to rejoice, even when it may seem challenging to do so. I ask this in the name of Jesus Christ. Amen."

Sit and begin meditating.

Breathe comfortably and make sure that you don't hold your breath at any time during the meditation.

Rest your hands open in your lap.

Listen to the inner promptings of the Holy Spirit.

To rejoice is to celebrate, and to rejoice always, as instructed in Philippians, is to maintain a positive attitude. This positivity isn't fake or superficial; it comes from a deep sense of faith. Replicate that in your life by celebrating wins and seeing things positively.

Describe in detail a past experience in which you received encouragement from the positivity of another person.

_____

_____

_____

_____

_____

_____

_____

_____

_____

_____

_____

_____

_____

_____

_____

_____

Describe in detail a past experience when you were able to provide encouragement and positivity for someone in a time when they needed it. What sentiment did you leave that experience with?

Speaking Life into the World

"A gentle tongue is a tree of life, but perverseness in it breaks the spirit."

Proverbs 15:4
English Standard Version

Prayer and Meditation

Say a brief prayer to set the intention for your meditation:

"Dear God, thank You for this day. Thank You for the great power You have given us, Your children, with the spoken word. May I be blessed with wisdom and gentleness in this meditation that my words may be blessed, that I may speak life into all those around me. Remove all corruption from my heart, mind, and tongue. I ask this in the name of Jesus Christ. Amen."

Get into a comfortable physical position and relax your body.

Take three deep inhales and exhales, then return to natural breathing.

Place your left hand on your heart and your right hand on your throat.

Visualize a rainbow light representing God's love and the spirit of everlasting life flowing from deep in your heart into your throat.

Maintain this visualization for a few minutes.

The goal with this meditation practice is to let go of the harsh unconscious speaking habits we have and begin to train ourselves to speak more lovingly and encouragingly to those around us.

Reflect on a time when you said something that incited a negative reaction in another. Write out loving, life-affirming alternatives that you can say in future similar circumstances.

Reflect on any negative self-talk you may have. Write out loving, life-affirming statements about yourself now to replace negative, spirit-breaking statements.

Section Nine

SELF-CONTROL

Taming the lower nature and inviting the Spirit's ways to become our own requires self-mastery and discipline. But we do not go on this journey alone. In this section we will saturate our minds and bodies with the great wisdom of self-control, in divine partnership with the Spirit, with promises of rewards in this world and beyond.

An Imperishable Reward

"Every athlete in training submits to strict discipline, in order to be crowned with a wreath that will not last; but we do it for one that will last forever."

1 Corinthians 9:25
Good News Translation

Prayer and Meditation

Say a brief prayer to set the intention for your meditation:

"Dear God, thank You for this day. May Your Holy Spirit be with me now as I meditate on the imperishable wreath of Your salvation. May I be granted with eternal perspective in the present that I may know Your ways more and more each day. Thank You for the journey You are leading me on, for I know that You love me and that You are always with me. I ask and pray all of this in the name of Jesus Christ. Amen."

Have a seat and let your body settle into a relaxed stillness.

Bring to mind the different material goals that you may have; awards, luxury goods, etc.

Envision those awards as they lose their luster after 10 years, 50 years, 250 years, until they eventually crumble into dust.

Silently repeat the sentence "God's glory is eternal and will never fade."

The physical world is full of idols, which are any kind of material possession that causes us to temporarily forget about the eternal goodness of God. As you journal, practice the spiritual perspective, rather than the material perspective that the world projects onto us.

What "idols" came to mind for you? Don't judge yourself for having material goals, just simply identify them here now. Describe what it would look like for those material possessions to crumble, decompose, and fade.

Describe a heavenly eternity beyond physical life wherein you are surrounded by your loved ones and free from suffering. Who is there with you? What kinds of limitations and suffering in the physical world are you now free of while in this celestial glory?

Fortress of Self-Control

"He that hath no rule over his own spirit is like a city that is broken down, and without walls."

Proverbs 25:28
King James Version

Prayer and Meditation

Say a brief prayer to set the intention for your meditation:

"Dear God, thank You for this day. Thank You for the protection and guidance You have provided me from the beginning. May my self-control be deepened and expanded in my meditation today. May my self-control create a field of safety around me in my life, that I may be as a fortress, and not as a city broken into and left without walls. Thank You for Your grace. I know that through You all things are possible. I ask and pray for these things in the name of Jesus Christ. Amen."

Sit comfortably and take a few deep breaths. Let your exhales release an audible sigh. After three to five breaths like this, return to natural breathing.

Visualize yourself in a variety of different clothing, different environments, and over time as you practice meditation, prayer, and scripture study.

Visualize yourself eating a variety of healthy meals, performing a variety of different physical exercises. Make them all as relatable as possible, visualizing them in your home, work, church, gym, neighborhood, etc.

Visualize these activities filling you with light that radiates in all directions around you, strengthening and protecting you both spiritually and physically.

What are three small changes you can make immediately to begin exercising greater self-control?

How can you use the light from this meditation to lift, inspire, and motivate yourself into better self-control?

Cultivating Wisdom and Health

"Before you speak, learn, and before you fall ill, take care of your health."

Sirach 18:19
Revised Standard Version

Prayer and Meditation

Say a brief prayer to set the intention for your meditation:

"Dear God, thank You for this day. Thank You for Your great wisdom. Thank You for Your Holy Spirit and Your son Jesus Christ. Bless me as I meditate today that I may deepen my self-control. Bless me that I may learn before I speak. Bless me that I may cultivate health to prevent falling ill. Bless me that as I meditate in Your presence, I will become more and more like You. I ask this in the name of Jesus Christ. Amen."

Set a timer for 15 to 20 minutes.

Sit comfortably and breathe naturally.

Rest your hands in whatever way feels comfortable for you.

Let your entire body be totally still for the duration of the meditation.

If possible, allow your only movement to be breath and heartbeat.

With every exhale, allow a wave of relaxation to pass through every muscle group in the body.

Today's practice is focused specifically on self-control in the form of cultivating and maintaining relaxed stillness.

Wisdom comes from maturity—not necessarily age. There are many young people wise beyond their years, and many older people who have arrested development and resist maturation.

How can you tune in to Christ's love to implement more self-awareness and control throughout your life?

The featured passage here specifically refers to our words and our health, giving them spiritual relevance. What does it mean for you to learn before you speak? What does it mean for you to cultivate health to prevent illness?

Resources

Practical Meditation for Beginners: 10 Days to a Happier, Calmer You by Benjamin W. Decker

The key to building a solid meditation practice is in the *practice* itself. From Zen and Vipassana to walking meditations and body scans, the simple practices outlined in *Practical Meditation for Beginners* make it easy to build an ongoing meditation routine that is best for you. Accessible and effective, *Practical Meditation for Beginners* is a true how-to guide that will empower you immediately to meditate with confidence. *Available everywhere books are sold.*

Unplug Guided Meditation App

Unplug Meditation in Los Angeles is the first drop-in, secular meditation studio in the world. Unplug features in-person and online classes with a wide variety of meditation techniques, guided experiences, and an inspirational daily email linking to a short meditation of the day. Unplug's guided meditation app is like having the studio in your pocket. *Unplug.com/online-classes*

The DEN Meditation

The DEN Meditation is a cross-disciplinary meditation studio in Los Angeles with multiple locations. Their online platform offers a variety of meditation workshops, classes, certifications, free meditations, and guided practices. The studio also features a podcast led by The DEN's founder. *DenAnywhere.com*

Daily Effective Prayer

This prayer media service hosts a YouTube channel offering an extensive list of Christian prayers for just about everything under the sun. It also has social media communities and accepts online prayer requests. *DailyEffectivePrayer.com*

Bible Gateway

Bible Gateway is a searchable online Bible in more than 200 versions and 70 languages that you can freely read, research, and reference anywhere. It features a library of audio Bibles, a mobile app, devotionals, e-mail newsletters, and other free resources. *BibleGateway.com*

Fireside Library and Meditation Center

This Library and Meditation Center features an extensive spiritual and religious research library, as well as an elaborate collection of anthropological and historical works. It's located within the historic First Unitarian Church of Los Angeles.

UULA.org

Acknowledgments

Great love and appreciation goes to my brothers, Andrew, Christopher, Chad, Jeffrey Scott, and Theo, as well as my loving sisters-in-law, Corey, Kendra, Mollie, and Mackenzie. Thank you for being loving examples and great pillars of support to me. Thank you for the inspiration, Jack, Charlie, Wyatt, Nolan, Lincoln, Audrey, and Henry, and all my future nieces and nephews who will reveal new spiritual truths and lead a generation to peace and great joy.

Thank you to the teachers and mentors who have kept me on the straight and narrow, while never making me feel judged or unloved, particularly to Marianne Williamson. Also to Russell M. Nelson, Judith Orloff, Corey Folsom, Deepak Chopra, Dr. Ronald Alexander, Sister Jenna, Gerard Powell, Wendy Zahler, David Kessler, Frances Fischer, Elaine Duncan, Bradley Wells, Brandee Sabella, Michael Beckwith, Bill Johnson, Jeff McNairy, Toure Roberts, Jennifer Sodini, Megan Monahan, Cassandra Bodzak, Sahara Rose, Christina Huntington, John Sahakian, Camilla Scare-Dallerup, Lauren Eckstrom, Chandresh Bhardwaj, Kyrstin Munson, Bryant Wood, Darcie Odom, Michael Morgan, Lauren Selsky, Felicia Tomasko, Keola Whittaker, Ansley Weller, Trinity Tran, Tandra Steiner, Marcia Cross and in sincerity to many whose names are not written here.

Thank you to Jonathan Ngai, Erica Greve, Jordan Wagner, AnnaLynne McCord, Sharon Ngai, Suze Yalof Schwartz, Jeff Krasno, Tal Rabinowitz, Jeffrey Segal, all of my family at Haven, and team at Lakanto.

My heart overflows with respect and gratitude for Camille Hayes, Joe Cho, Andrea Leptinsky, Rochelle Torke, Gemma Capdevila, and my team at Rock Ridge Press.

Deep love extends to my brother, Jesus Christ, for being with me since the beginning, through thick and thin, with nothing but love and generosity.

About the Author

Once praised by *Forbes* magazine as a "legendary Hollywood PR maven," Benjamin W. Decker left a prolific career as an entertainment industry executive in pursuit of "more meaningful work." Today, he is a meditation teacher, social activist, and author of *Practical Meditation for Beginners: 10 Days to a Happier, Calmer You*. Decker is a founding meditation teacher at Unplug Meditation and The DEN Meditation in Los Angeles, as well as the founding Spiritual Director of Full Circle Venice. He's also the founding director of partnerships at Unlikely Heroes, an anti-human-trafficking organization; the former director of partnerships at Generosity.org, a humanitarian aid organization; and founder of the Fireside Library and Meditation Center at the First Unitarian Church of Los Angeles. He is a descendant of the founding pioneer families of The Church of Jesus Christ of Latter-Day Saints and is lifelong Christian with an unshakeable testimony of the living Christ.